Villiam Bolcom

Romanza

for Solo Violin and String Orchestra

PIANO REDUCTION

1. Romanza

2. Valse funèbre

3. Cakewalk

ISBN 978-1-4584-1908-8

EDWARD B.
MARKS MUSIC
COMPANY

Exclusively Distributed By

HAL•LEONARD®
CORPORATION
7777 W. BLUEMOUND RD. P.O. BOX 13819 MILWAUKEE, WI 53213

www.ebmarks.com
www.halleonard.com

for Nadja

Romanza

for solo violin and string orchestra

WILLIAM BOLCOM
2009

I. Romanza

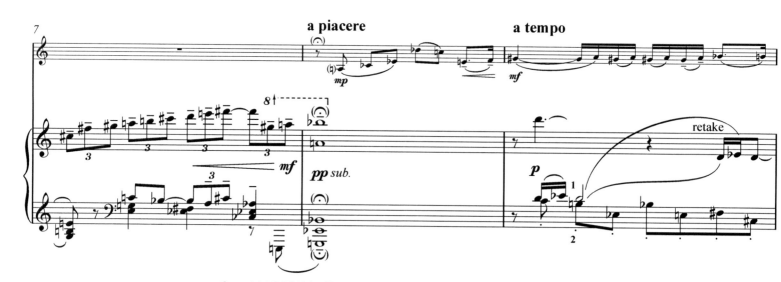

* trattenuto: a slight stretching of the tempo.

7

12

Solo Violin

for Nadja
Romanza
for solo violin and string orchestra

WILLIAM BOLCOM
2009

I. Romanza

* trattenuto: a slight stretching of the tempo.

TIME

II. Valse funèbre

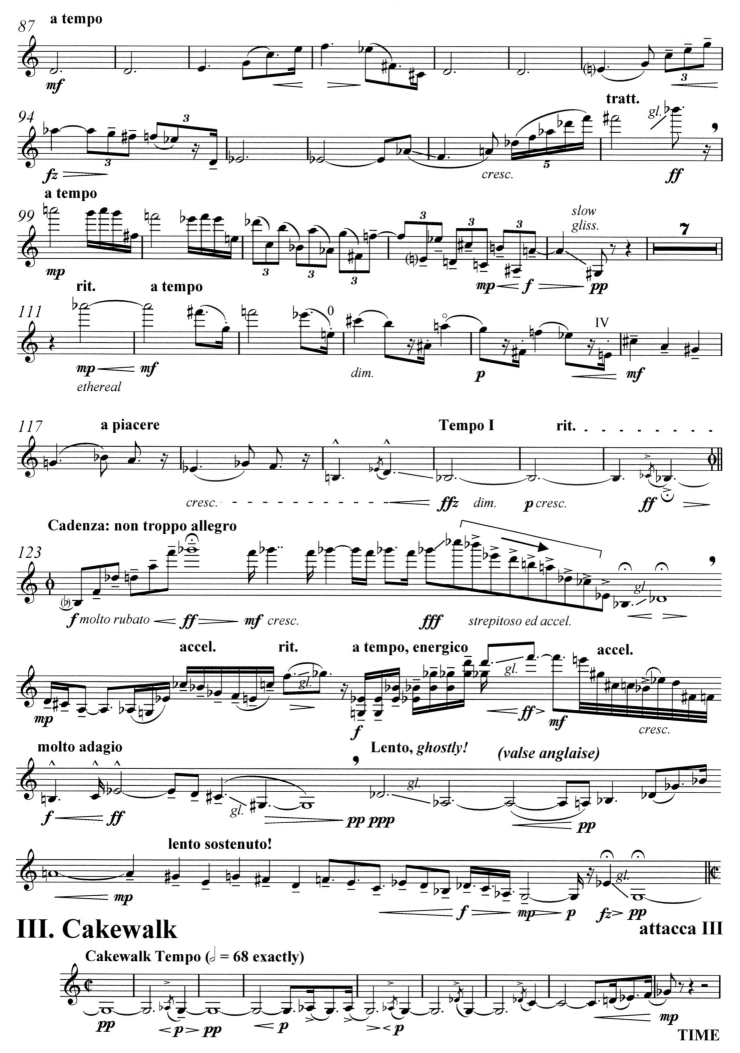

III. Cakewalk

attacca III

II. Valse funèbre

Sostenuto; *misterioso* (♩ = c. 84)

attacca III

III. Cakewalk

Cakewalk Tempo (♩ = 68 exactly)

William Bolcom
Violin Works

U.S. $17.99

HL00220365

ISBN 978-1-4584-1908-8